BEVERLY K. DUNCAN

EXPLORE the WILD

A NATURE SEARCH-AND-FIND BOOK

HarperCollins*Publishers*

For my grandmother, Rosena Kathleen,
who painted the deserts of
southern California so beautifully

EXPLORE THE WILD
A Nature Search-and-Find Book
Copyright © 1996 by Beverly K. Duncan
All rights reserved. No part of this book may be used or reproduced
in any manner whatsoever without written permission except in the case of
brief quotations embodied in critical articles and reviews. Printed in the United
States of America. For information address HarperCollins Children's Books, a
division of HarperCollins Publishers, 10 East 53rd Street, New York, NY 10022.

Library of Congress Cataloging-in-Publication Data
Duncan, Beverly K., date
  Explore the wild : a nature search-and-find book / Beverly K. Duncan.
    p.   cm.
  ISBN 0-06-023596-9. — ISBN 0-06-023597-7 (lib. bdg.)
  1. Natural history—United States—Juvenile literature. 2. Habitat (Ecology)—
United States—Juvenile literature. [1. Habitat (Ecology) 2. Natural history.
3. Ecology.] I. Title.
QH104.D78 1996   93-43909
574.5'0973—dc20   CIP
                                                                                          AC

Typography by Elynn Cohen
1   2   3   4   5   6   7   8   9   10
❖
First Edition

AUTHOR'S NOTE

Seven different environments that exist in the United States are presented in this book. As I researched each of these habitats, I learned about the characteristics of each place and about the plants and animals that live there. It became more and more exciting as I began to understand how these plants and animals have adapted to unique conditions in order to survive.

So that you can explore these habitats in *Explore the Wild: A Nature Search-and-Find Book*, I've painted pictures of the seven environments, and preceding each of these pictures I've included key pages. The key pages will give you information about the environments and their inhabitants. And, to help you find and identify plants and animals as you search through the main paintings, there are close-up pictures of each in the key pages.

Though I have tried to paint the environments in a realistic manner, I have taken artistic license by placing so many plants and animals in each habitat. In reality, a person would not see so many at once. Nor would a person see, at the same time, animals that are active during the day together with those active only at night. But to create pictures in which you could search and make discoveries, I felt that I should paint very full scenes.

Beverly Duncan

DESERT OF THE SOUTHWEST

Although the desert is hot and dry most of the year, a great number of plants and animals live here. They've adapted to the harsh climate in a variety of ways. Many of the animals are active only during the early morning, late afternoon, or night to escape the scorching midday heat. During the hottest and driest times, some animals and most plants go into a resting state called dormancy. Furthermore, plant leaves, which lose water through evaporation, are small or wax covered to slow water loss. Cactus leaves have become spines for the same reason. Only after the spring rains, which last for six to ten weeks, do the subtle, dry colors of the desert change to richer tones.

Roadrunner—This large bird, also called the snake bird or the ground cuckoo, is often seen running along the ground. Chasing insects, snakes, or lizards, it changes direction abruptly with a lift of its tail or wing. Because its wings are weak, it can fly only short distances.

Cholla Cactus—Many desert dwellers live among the spiny joints of this treelike cactus.

White-Winged Dove—Nesting on the saguaro, this small dove eats nectar from its flowers and enjoys its fruit later in the summer.

Whiptail Lizard—This slender, long-tailed lizard is one of the speediest of all desert lizards. It digs out its prey—insects, spiders, and scorpions—from the sand.

Gila Monster—Generally slow and sluggish, this is the largest lizard of North America. Growing up to 2 feet long, it spends most of the year underground away from heat or cold. The only poisonous lizard in the United States, it is not likely to bite unless provoked. Its venom causes pain but rarely human death.

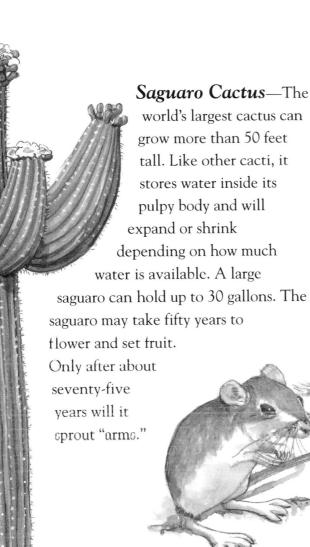

Saguaro Cactus—The world's largest cactus can grow more than 50 feet tall. Like other cacti, it stores water inside its pulpy body and will expand or shrink depending on how much water is available. A large saguaro can hold up to 30 gallons. The saguaro may take fifty years to flower and set fruit. Only after about seventy-five years will it sprout "arms."

Red-Tailed Hawk—Known also as the hen or chicken hawk, this large bird often nests on the "arm" of a saguaro.

Kangaroo Rat—This hopping rat is perhaps the creature most perfectly adapted to desert life. It does not need to drink water, but gets moisture from the seeds, grasses, and cactus pulp that it eats. It spends much of the day in cooler, underground sealed burrows, which help it conserve moisture.

Desert Primrose—The seed of this flower lies dormant underground until the rains come.

Elf Owl—Just five inches high, this is the smallest owl in the world. It generally nests in holes in the saguaro, which have been carved out by the gila woodpecker. These holes are cooler than the outside air because the cactus walls are thick and moist.

Tarantula—The venom of this large, slow-moving spider is lethal only to small creatures like insects, though it can cause swelling and itching in people.

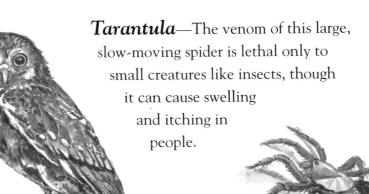

5

Cactus Wren—This bird constructs a woven, flask-shaped nest with a spiny entrance in the cholla cactus. It runs or flies close to the ground, catching spiders and insects.

Gila Woodpecker—The chisellike beak of this bird pecks nest holes in the saguaro, which are later used by other desert animals.

Hummingbird—Hummingbirds are the smallest of all birds. They eat insects and nectar from cactus flowers.

Cactus Beetle Nymph—This immature insect sucks juices from plants.

Coyote—An adaptive animal, the coyote thrives in many different environments. Even in the desert it has no trouble finding food. It generally spends the day in the shade, hunting only when it is cooler.

Yucca—This member of the lily family is pollinated only by the female yucca moth, who does so at night when she lays eggs within each flower. Native Americans have long used parts of this plant in many ways. They've eaten the roots, flowers, and seeds; made rope out of fiber from the leaves; and made soap from the plant juices.

Horned Lizard—Also called a horned toad, this little lizard escapes predators and heat by wiggling from side to side into an insulating blanket of sand. It especially likes to eat ants, devouring up to sixty-three in a half hour.

Desert Tortoise—This animal uses its curved claws to dig its way underground, where it spends up to nine months of the year, avoiding heat and cold. Sacs located just underneath its shell store extra water for dry periods.

Barrel Cactus—This cactus can be a few inches to 10 feet high. It produces long, hooked spines that have been used as fishhooks by Native Americans.

Prickly Pear Cactus—The spiny pads of this cactus may turn purple during times of drought or cold weather.

Western Diamondback Rattlesnake   This is the most poisonous creature of the desert. When disturbed, this snake stands its ground and shakes a rattle at the end of its body. A new section of the rattle is added each time the snake sheds its skin.

Pack Rat—This animal uses cholla cactus joints and other cactus spines to protect its nest on the ground.

Ocotillo—Popularly called "candlewood" or "flamewood" due to its red flowers, the ocotillo sheds its leaves during dry periods to slow evaporation.

Desert Lily—Soon after the rains this lily blooms, living only long enough to store food in its underground bulb for the next year's bloom.

Western Banded Gecko—At dusk this lizard emerges from hiding to hunt beetles and other small prey. Unlike most lizards, it squeaks when bothered.

7

DESERT OF THE SOUTHWEST

GRASSLAND OF THE MIDWEST

On the grassland or prairie of the Midwest, summers are hot and dry and winters are cold and harsh. The grasses and plants that grow on this open land have wide, deep, fast-growing root systems. One half of a grass's growth is below ground in the rich soil. This sturdy root system is not harmed when prairie animals eat the leafy growth, or even when fires sweep over the land. Plant stalks are flexible so they bend, but don't break, in the winds. There are few trees, and birds nest on or under the ground. Some animals live underground too, since it is cooler there in summer and warmer in winter. They can also escape fires by going underground. The rains that usually come twice a year, in the spring and fall, ensure healthy growth for the grasses and herbs that form the grassland.

Black-Tailed Prairie Dog—This animal lives in large family "towns" that consist of underground burrows and chambers covering hundreds of acres. A sharp bark from an alert "dog" standing aboveground sends all others in the area diving down and out of danger.

Little Bluestem—With a dense root system that reaches 5 to 8 feet deep, this is one of the most widely distributed grasses in America. It's also a very nutritious food for prairie animals.

Black Samson—The center "cone" of this flower stays on and turns black after the petals fall off.

Swift Fox—This smallest member of the fox family is the size of a house cat. It digs dens underground, often enlarging burrows already hollowed out by other, smaller animals. Once hunted for its fur, the swift fox is making a comeback on the prairie after nearly becoming extinct.

Pronghorn Antelope—The fastest animal of North America, this member of the deer family can outrun most predators. With vision as keen as five-power binoculars, it can spot danger from a great distance across the open land. It has a stomach specially developed to digest the tough fibers of the prairie grasses.

Burrowing Owl—Though this small owl can dig its own tunnels, it generally nests in an abandoned prairie dog burrow. It often stands at the burrow entrance during the day, scanning the land and sky for predators and its favorite food, flying insects.

Stiff Goldenrod—
This deep-rooted plant flowers in the fall.

Deer Mouse—This rodent is the favorite prey of the prairie rattlesnake.

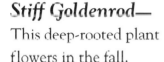

Great Spangled Fritillary—
A common butterfly of the grassland, this insect pollinates flowers.

Prairie Rattlesnake—During the summer this poisonous snake hunts its favorite prey, the deer mouse. When temperatures drop and days get shorter, it returns to its den, where it hibernates for the winter.

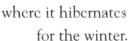

Dotted Gayfeather—
This colorful plant has deep roots, and blooms in the fall.

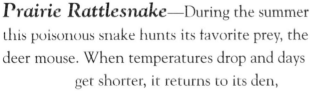

Western Meadowlark—
This bird builds a loose grassy structure on the ground for its nest. It migrates south for the winter.

Killdeer—This bird nests on the ground at the bases of grasses and around the mounds of the prairie dog burrows. A mother will pretend to have a broken wing and run to lure a predator away from her nest.

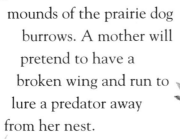

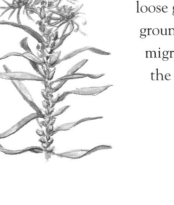

Differential Grasshopper—
This insect eats grass. Thousands of these grasshoppers will sometimes swarm across the land, stripping the prairie of its grasses.

Honeybee—This insect is important for the pollination of grassland flowers.

Plains Spadefoot Toad—This toad spends the hot part of the day backed into a burrow, which it digs with a spade-shaped part of its hind feet.

Maximilian Sunflower—This tall plant has flowers that turn toward the sun as it moves across the sky. It produces a lot of seeds, which prairie birds like to eat.

Needlegrass—Also known as porcupine grass, this prairie grass has seeds that fall to the ground, twisting and screwing themselves into the soil, where they can then sprout and grow.

Bison—Also known as the buffalo, this is the largest land animal of North America. It may grow as tall as seven feet at the shoulder. Bison are wild cattle, related to the antelope and deer, and have special stomachs to digest the grasses. There were once so many thousands in a herd that the group would take days to pass one point.

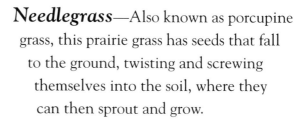

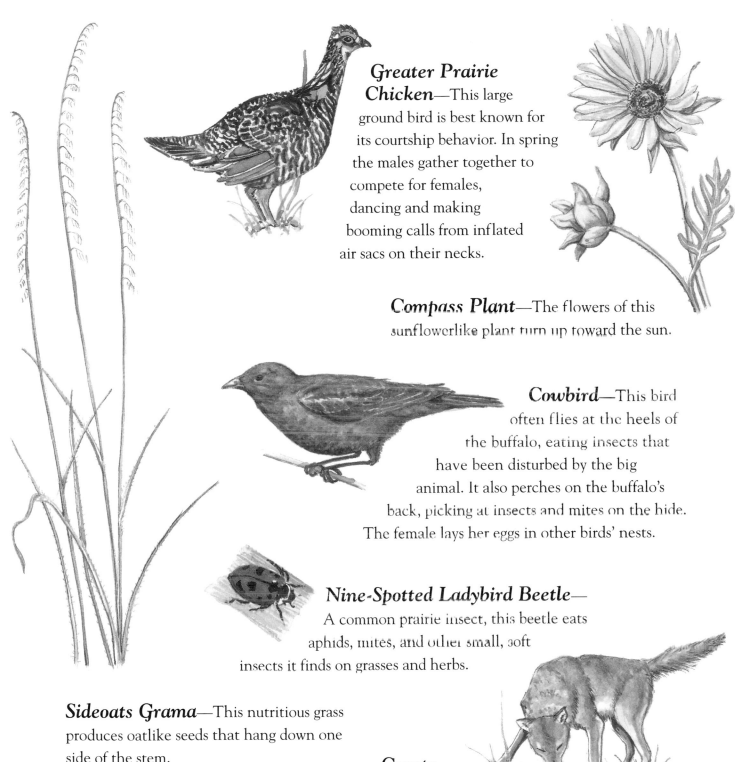

Greater Prairie Chicken—This large ground bird is best known for its courtship behavior. In spring the males gather together to compete for females, dancing and making booming calls from inflated air sacs on their necks.

Compass Plant—The flowers of this sunflowerlike plant turn up toward the sun.

Cowbird—This bird often flies at the heels of the buffalo, eating insects that have been disturbed by the big animal. It also perches on the buffalo's back, picking at insects and mites on the hide. The female lays her eggs in other birds' nests.

Nine-Spotted Ladybird Beetle— A common prairie insect, this beetle eats aphids, mites, and other small, soft insects it finds on grasses and herbs.

Sideoats Grama—This nutritious grass produces oatlike seeds that hang down one side of the stem.

Coyote— This adaptive animal digs out dens in other animals' burrows. It preys upon whatever is available, including insects, lizards, mice, rabbits, and swift fox young.

Prairie Horned Lark— Preferring open, even barren land, this lark will build a grass nest near a stone or clod of earth.

13

GRASSLAND OF THE MIDWEST

ALPINE TUNDRA OF THE ROCKY MOUNTAINS

The plants and animals that live above the tree line, in the high country of the Rocky Mountains, have resourcefully adapted to challenging environmental conditions. Plants are small and lie close to the ground to avoid high winds and to trap heat. Their growth is limited to the seven or eight weeks of summer between a late thaw and an early frost. Because there is very little rainfall, they have long taproots that find water deep among the rocks. Animals have had to adapt to the lower oxygen levels at these higher elevations. Their hearts beat faster to pump more oxygen through their bodies. Those that live here year-round must prepare for the long winters. Some gather and store food; others eat and store fat in their bodies. The short alpine summer is a burst of color and life as plants reproduce and grow, and animals mate, raise young, and prepare for the rest of the year.

Moss—This nonflowering plant needs water to make food. When water is unavailable, it folds or curls up to prevent evaporation.

Crane Fly—
A common prey of insect-eating birds, the crane fly lays its eggs in moist areas, often on moss.

Kobresia—
Mountain goats, pikas, and marmots eat this very nutritious grasslike plant. Rather than sending out fresh green growth from its base, it grows from the brown end of last year's growth. A reddish ring separates each year's growth.

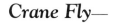

Mountain Harebell—
This dwarfed alpine plant is also known as a bluebell or a bellflower.

Rocky Mountain Goat—This member of the antelope family is one of the most sure-footed mountain animals in the world. It has specialized hoofs with hard edges and rubbery, suctionlike inner pads. It lives on grasses, leaves, moss, and lichen.

Pika—This relative of the rabbit has small ears set close to its head to protect them from frostbite. During the short summer it cuts, dries, and stores up to a bushel of alpine vegetation for winter, thus earning the nickname "haymaker of the mountains."

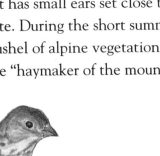

Brown-Capped Rosy Finch—
An insect eater, this finch is one of the few birds that migrates into this habitat to nest and raise its young.

Dwarf Clover—Another plant that has adapted to this environment by growing low to the ground, it spreads by sending out stems that take root.

Common Ground Beetle—Like many alpine beetles, this one's black color helps it absorb as much heat as possible during the warmth of the summer.

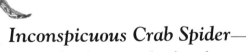

Inconspicuous Crab Spider—
This spider changes color from brown and red to yellow and gray to match the color of its surroundings.

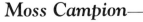

Moss Campion—
Only two inches high, this plant forms a tight, rock-hugging mound to trap heat and windblown soil. Like many alpine plants, it grows slowly, only a half inch in width in five years.

Snowball Saxifrage—To take advantage of the short growing season, this little plant sends up new leaves and a flower ready for pollination in five days.

Alpine Forget-Me-Not—
This plant grows no more than 4 inches high in the alpine habitat, while it may grow 12 inches in another environment. Hair on its leaves and stems helps trap heat.

Golden Northern Bumblebee—This bee visits the alpine tundra on sunny days, pollinating the flowers.

White-Crowned Sparrow—A seed eater, this bird nests here in the summer but migrates elsewhere for winter.

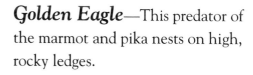

Golden Eagle—This predator of the marmot and pika nests on high, rocky ledges.

Lubber Grasshopper—
Like all grasshoppers of the alpine tundra, this one may take up to three years to mature instead of the usual one year due to the short "growing," or summer, season.

Western Two-Spotted Ladybug Beetle—A predator of smaller insects, this beetle spends the winter under leaves, bark, and rocks, often in clusters with other ladybug beetles.

Rock-Slide Daisy—
Often found growing in loose rock, this daisy has a long, stout taproot—2 to 5 feet deep—to reach a water source.

Clark's Nutcracker—
This daytime visitor hides pine seeds found below alpine country among the rocks. It will revisit these sites when it needs food.

Alpine Sorrel—This little plant grows in wet, rocky places.

Dwarf Columbine—
The alpine version of this common wildflower is smaller than plants found in less severe environments.

Little Black Ant—Like most ants, this one lives in an underground colony with others, working together to raise young and gather food.

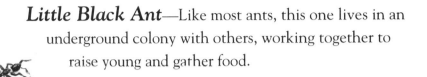

Wolf Spider—In the summer this creature preys on insects that have been numbed by late-afternoon cold.

Yellow-Bellied Marmot—
During the summer this large rodent eats huge quantities of vegetation, storing fat in its body in order to survive the long winter hibernation. Both the marmot and pika make a barking sound whenever danger threatens.

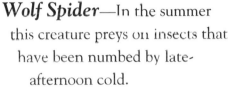

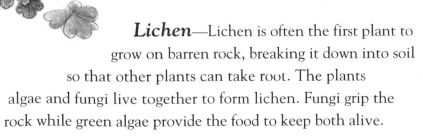

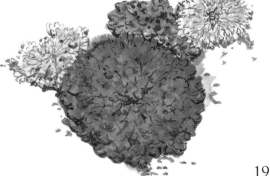

Lichen—Lichen is often the first plant to grow on barren rock, breaking it down into soil so that other plants can take root. The plants algae and fungi live together to form lichen. Fungi grip the rock while green algae provide the food to keep both alive.

ALPINE TUNDRA OF THE ROCKY MOUNTAINS

THE ARCTIC

The cold, ice-covered areas of northern Alaska at the edge of the sea are anything but lifeless. One type of plant, algae, grows just under the surface of the ice. A large group of algae can tint the snow a reddish color. A variety of animals thrive under these extreme conditions. In early June the sun never sets, temperatures rise above freezing, and the ice begins to melt. Noisy summer visitors, especially seabirds, arrive. They and the year-round inhabitants take advantage of the large supply of food in the sea to eat, nest, and raise young. The polar bear, arctic wolf, and arctic fox use floating ice as stepping stones to get to prey. In late August temperatures drop below freezing, and ice begins to form again. The Arctic becomes quiet as summer visitors fly or swim south, leaving only a few hardy animals with thick coats of fur or feathers to survive the long, dark winter.

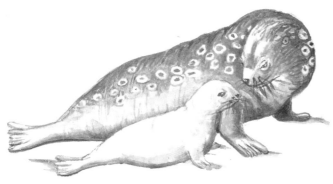

Ermine—Also called a weasel, this small animal has white fur in the winter and brown fur in the summer. It is a quick, fierce predator, often tackling animals larger than itself.

Ringed Seal—Traveling farther north than any other mammal, this seal hunts under the ice for fish and shrimp. It can stay underwater for seven or eight minutes, but must come up to breathe at an airhole in the ice—where a polar bear may be waiting.

Orange-Golden Bumblebee—During the summer this insect may be temporarily blown onto the ice from surrounding land.

Arctic Wolf—One of the few enemies of the arctic fox, this wolf is active year round.

Ice Worm—This black threadlike worm lives in the top 4 to 6 inches of snow on the surface of the ice, feeding on red algae and bits of pollen that blow in.

Long-Tailed Jaeger—This seabird migrates here for the summer. It chases gulls and terns, trying to steal food in midair.

Krill—This tiny, shrimplike animal is very nutritious. Thousands at a time make a meal for the humpback whales and other forms of sea life that visit the Arctic during the summer.

Snow Mosquito—This insect is often blown onto the ice from neighboring forest breeding grounds. Unlike other mosquitoes, it is active in the cold of early spring and able to lay eggs in pools of melting snow.

Polar Bear—One of the largest land carnivores in the world, the polar bear spends its life on the ice or near the coast, hunting seals. It can swim up to one hundred miles at one time without stopping. The dense, oily fur keeps out the cold of winter and ocean waters. Its hairs are transparent, hollow tubes that trap heat and reflect back the color white. The skin underneath is black to absorb more heat from the sun.

Snow Bunting—This land bird flies north for the summer to nest on the neighboring tundra. It eats the glacier worm.

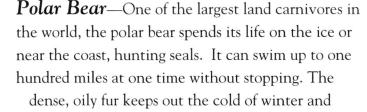

Glaucous Gull— A summer visitor, this seabird feeds on bear kills.

Orca— Also called the killer whale, this mammal comes to the Arctic in the summer to hunt. One of the ways it preys on seals is by bumping them off the ice.

Snow Flea— This tiny, wingless insect is found on the surface of the snow. It freezes overnight as temperatures drop. When its dark-brown body has absorbed enough warmth again, it will jump over the ice in search of algae, pollen, and dead insects.

Arctic Tern— This seabird and summer visitor snatches fish from the ocean's surface and eats as it flies.

Gyrfalcon— This falcon rarely travels out of the Arctic. It preys on seabirds, land birds, arctic hares, and other small animals.

Arctic Fox— Ice is the home year-round for this fox, which is not much bigger than a house cat. During the summer it stores extra prey—eggs, birds, and small mammals—in shallow holes where the food freezes for winter. It follows the polar bear over the ice in the winter to scavenge what is left of the bear's seal kills.

Red Phalarope— This shorebird migrates north for the summer. By paddling on the water in a circle, it creates a force that draws food to the surface.

Arctic Hare—Active year-round, this animal eats frozen plant shoots from the neighboring arctic tundra during the winter.

Ivory Gull—This rare seabird comes north to breed and feed in the constant light of the Arctic sun. It scavenges on bear kills, eating even the blood-soaked snow.

Migratory Grasshopper During the summer, this insect is often blown by strong winds onto the ice, where it will probably die or be eaten by another animal.

Harp Seal— This seal migrates from the south each summer to feed on fish and other sea life at the edge of the ice.

Water Pipit—A summer visitor, this land bird nests in nearby tundra. It eats seeds and insects that have blown onto the ice.

THE ARCTIC

KELP FOREST OF THE PACIFIC COAST

Many creatures live in the dim light of the kelp forest off the California coast. The giant sea kelp grows here, in cool, nutrient-rich waters. It is the biggest of all sea plants and the world's largest alga, growing up to two hundred feet high, from the ocean floor to the water's surface. Its flexible stalks and "leaves" sway with the ocean currents instead of snapping off. Gas-filled floats at the base of each "leaf" keep the plant floating so that it doesn't drop to the ocean floor under its own weight. Animals live on or among the kelp roots, stalks, and "leaves," finding food and safe hiding places from predators. All life in this habitat is dependent in some way on the giant sea kelp.

Strawberry Anemone— Looking a bit like the fruit for which it is named, this anemone uses its petallike tentacles to sting prey.

Sea Otter—This curious, playful water creature is important for a healthy kelp forest because it eats the kelp's greatest natural enemy, the purple sea urchin. The otter wraps kelp leaves loosely around its body before resting so that it doesn't drift away with the tides. The leaves also hide it from predators.

Bat Star— This sea star is a predator of sea urchins, among other animals. It has many suction pads on its arms, and like all sea stars it feeds by turning its stomach inside out to envelop and digest its prey.

Rough Keyhole Limpet— Like most limpets, this one eats algae that grow on rocks. It protects itself from sea stars by covering itself with a slippery coating, which a star's sucker arms cannot grip.

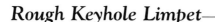

Gorgonian Coral—This bushlike animal waits for microscopic creatures to float by within reach of its stinging "hairs."

Kelp Snail—This underwater snail eats a layer of cells off the kelp as it travels up the plant. When it reaches the top, it drops off, falling to the ocean floor to begin its climb again.

Blood Sea Star—This is one of many sea stars living in the kelp forest. Like other sea stars, it is able to grow another arm if one is lost to a predator.

Squid—This 6-inch squid can change the color of its body to match the colors around it. In the spring after mating, the females lay thousands of egg cases, which look like white rice and cover the ocean floor. Then the adult squids die, becoming food for many other animals of the kelp forest.

Pelagic Red Crab—This crab lives and feeds on parts of the kelp.

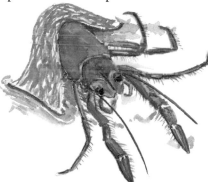

Blue Shark—This shark waits just beyond the kelp for prey to venture out from the protection of the forest. Like all sharks, it has a skeleton of cartilage rather than bone, very good hearing, and an excellent sense of smell.

Sea Anemone—Though they sometimes look like lovely ocean flowers, these animals have tentacles that can sting. The tentacles stun prey—small fish, crabs, or snails—and move it to the anemone's central mouth.

Garibaldi—This brilliantly colored fish is highly visible among the kelp leaves. Predators have discovered that it tastes terrible and so have learned to stay away.

Rockfish—The reddish markings of this fish help it blend into the dappled light of the kelp forest.

Giant Sea Kelp—Called the "sea otter's cradle," this alga is used by the mother otter to hold and hide her baby while she hunts for food. It is the fastest growing plant in the world, shooting up as much as two feet a day. An individual stalk may live only five or six months, then separate from the roots and float away. The roots, however, may live for ten years, producing new shoots for the kelp forest. Ocean storms can cause violent currents, which rip up entire forests of stalks. Yet the roots will begin new growth and within a year produce a new forest.

Purple Sea Urchin—One of several types of urchins that live in the kelp forest, this is the greatest natural enemy of the kelp plant. The purple sea urchin will eat only the kelp leaves when predators keep its numbers down. When its numbers increase too much, it will eat the kelp roots, killing the plant.

Octopus—This creature is small and slippery like a bar of soap. It is a master of camouflage, taking on the color and texture of its surroundings in a second. To escape danger, it can swim backward at very fast speeds. It can also squirt out an inky substance that dulls the senses of a predator.

Kelpfish—This fish hides among the kelp while it searches for food. Its shape and color are similar to kelp leaves, making camouflage easy.

Spanish Shawl Nudibranch—
Predators stay away from this tiny,
brightly colored sea slug because
it tastes terrible. It feeds on
the tentacles of anemones,
transferring their
stinging cells
to its pretty
"quills."

Gobi—Like
the Garibaldi,
this colorful
fish does not
need to hide from
predators because of its
terrible taste.

Sea Lion—This mammal hunts for
fish among the kelp.

Bat Ray—These rays, with wingspans of over
5 feet, meet each summer in clearings of the
kelp forest to mate. A relative of the shark,
bat rays usually swim near the ocean bottom,
feeding on other fish, shellfish, and worms.

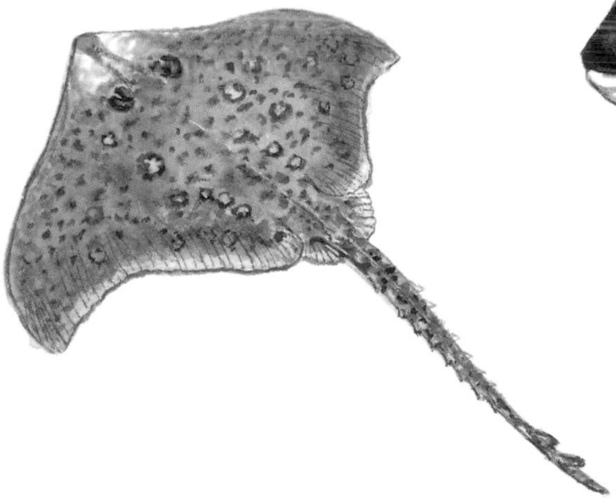

Sheepshead—
Using its big front teeth,
the sheepshead nibbles away the prickly
spines of sea urchins to reach their meat.
Along with the sea otter, it helps keep
down the number of purple sea urchins.

Harbor Seal—This seal rarely hunts
in the kelp forest but does rest among
the leaves near the surface, hiding
from the shark, its most dangerous enemy.

KELP FOREST OF THE PACIFIC COAST

SALT MARSH OF THE ATLANTIC COAST

Ocean waters meet the land at a salt or tidal marsh. Cordgrass grows here at the edge of the sea. Its roots trap drifting soil and stabilize the earth. This grass has adapted to living in salt water by developing special glands to get rid of excess salt. At high tide nutrient-rich ocean water floods the land. Large fish and other sea life may visit the marsh at this time while land animals step back to higher ground. Many marine animals feed on the fresh supply of microscopic life brought in by the sea. At low tide the marsh is laid bare to sun, wind, and rain. The animals that fed at high tide close up tightly and burrow in the mud to stay moist, while land animals move in to hunt for food. Life in the salt marsh continually responds to the endless cycle of the tides.

Barnacle—When it is very young, this creature permanently attaches itself to a hard surface. Its feelers push tiny seaweed pieces into its mouth at high tide. At low tide it closes up tightly so that it doesn't dry out.

Blue Crab—This crab spends the summer in shallow marsh waters, preying on clams and smaller crabs with its powerful pincers.

Muskrat—This creature nests among the grasses above the high-tide level. It eats mainly grasses and roots, though it may also eat fish and young birds.

Flounder—When a flounder is about one inch long, its left eye moves to the right side of its head. It can then see while lying on its side in the sand or mud, hiding from predators. Like other salt marsh creatures, this fish has kidneys and gills that are specially adapted so that it can live where salt and fresh water mix.

Red-Winged Blackbird—This bird often builds a hanging-basket nest from the grasses a few feet above the water line. It eats insects during the warmer seasons and seeds during the winter.

34

Common Northern Whelk— This scavenger feeds on the mud at low tide.

Clapper Rail— Because it is so shy, this common marsh bird is rarely seen by people. The expression "thin as a rail" comes from the way it quietly slips through the grass. It nests on the ground above high-tide levels. At low tide it catches fiddler crabs, insects, and seeds.

Hermit Crab—This underwater crab has a soft, curved back end. It searches for an empty snail shell to back into for its "home." As it grows, it moves into larger shells.

Seaside Sparrow—This sparrow lives only on salt marshes. It wades in shallow water, catching crabs and other small marine animals left in the mud at low tide.

Atlantic Ribbed Mussel—This mussel lives half buried in the mud. It attaches itself to the bottom of the cordgrass with strong threads that it "spins" so that rough tides will not shake it loose. At high tide it opens its shell and filters tiny bits of plants and animals into its body. At low tide it closes up tightly so that it doesn't dry out inside.

Cordgrass—Also called spartina, this highly nutritious grass sends out long, spreading roots that catch drifting dirt to form a firm base for the salt marsh. It grows from 4 inches to 7 feet tall and provides safe cover for both land and marine animals. In early morning or late afternoon, this plant glistens as the low light passes over excess salt crystals it has released through the special glands along its blades.

Atlantic Slipper Shell—This shell lives in chains; up to nine individuals pile on top of one another in shallow water where the bottom is muddy.

American Horsefly—This fly is a pest of the salt marsh, giving animals painful bites as it sucks their blood. Its larvae live and feed on rotting matter in the mud.

Atlantic Jackknife Clam—Because of its shape, this clam can burrow vertically into the mud at great speeds, escaping predators such as seagulls and people. It lives in the mud, and at high tide it sends a feeding tube up into the water to suck in small food particles.

Sea Lettuce—This alga grows in shallow waters, where it can get a lot of sunlight. Strong waves may rip it from the rocks and wash it into the salt marsh, where it becomes food for some animals.

Black-Necked Stilt—This bird heaps branches and grasses together to form a nest on the ground. It feeds on the small animals it finds at low tide.

Fiddler Crab—The fiddler crab has developed primitive lungs so it can stay out of water for several weeks. At low tide large groups of this half-inch crab move over the exposed mud searching for food and mates. The male has one large claw called the "fiddle," which it uses to attract females, waving it back and forth and bumping it on the ground.

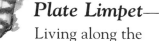

Plate Limpet—
Living along the
northern Atlantic coast,
this limpet grazes algae off
rocks. Its empty shell may be
washed to beaches and marshes
further south.

Woody Glasswort—
This plant was named
glasswort because in the
past people made glass
from its ashes. Like
those of cordgrass, its
roots help stabilize the
mud base of the marsh. It has
thick, waxy leaves and stems
to store water, which ocean
salt takes
out of plants.

Northern Quahog—This
clam burrows into the mud. At
high tide it extends its feeding
tube to collect small food
particles from the water.

Salt Marsh Periwinkle—At low
tide this snail hides under the cordgrass. At
high tide it climbs the grass, scraping off algae
as it stays above the water line.

Common Periwinkle—This snail
grazes algae off mussel shells.

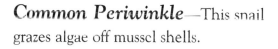

Moonsnail—This snail eats
a clam by drilling a hole in the shell with a raspy
mouth part and scraping out the meat.

Horseshoe Crab—This crab can
grow up to 28 inches long. It burrows in
mud and sand, hunting for worms and other
small animals. It is relatively unchanged
since the time of the dinosaurs.

Sand Dollar—
A flatter relative of the
sea urchin, the sand
dollar lives in sandier
underwater areas along the
coast. Its empty, smooth shell is often
found on beaches and marshes.

SALT MARSH OF THE ATLANTIC COAST

SWAMP OF THE SOUTHEAST

Large areas of land in the Southeast are divided by warm, shallow, slow-moving waterways. This area is called the "land of the trembling earth" because some of the islands are very unstable. Composed of peat—partially decayed plant material—the land is spongy and loose. Bits may float away until larger plants and trees take root, firming up the earth. One such tree, the bald cypress, has become an important part of this wet environment. It grows in the water and its swollen trunk base and spreading roots stabilize the tree and then the land. Many of the animals here use both water and land for shelter, food, and nesting sites. The alligator, for instance, nests on land near the water's edge and basks on the land in the sun, but hunts for food in the water. Plants and animals of the swamp have adjusted in their own ways to this part-land, part-water environment.

Arrow Arum—Large arrow-shaped leaves give this plant its name. It grows in moist soil where land and water meet.

American Bald Cypress—Sometimes called the swamp cypress, this stately tree grows in water. Its swollen base, often three to four times bigger around than the rest of the tree, stabilizes it in the water and on the spongy ground beneath. The roots grow out horizontally and sprout "knees," which are hollow and covered with bark. These knees allow the tree roots to breathe in low-oxygen, water-logged ground.

Rough Green Snake—Living in vines, bushes, and trees near water, this snake hunts for grasshoppers, crickets, caterpillars, and spiders. It swims well and may take to the water when disturbed.

Little Blue Heron—This medium-sized heron is a wading bird that hunts in swamp waters.

Purple Gallinule—Long toes enable this beautifully colored water bird to walk across lily pads and other water plants as it searches for food. It eats small water animals, eggs, and some seeds.

Green Heron—Growing up to 22 inches long, this wading bird hunts by waiting quietly, motionless, until prey is within reach. It will then quickly stab with its pointed bill, trying to catch small fish, frogs, lizards, and snakes.

Southeastern Lubber Grasshopper—This short-winged grasshopper perches on swamp plants, eating the leaves.

Florida Cooter—Living and hunting in water near the land, this turtle may crawl onto a log to lie in the sun. The female lays her eggs in abandoned alligator nests. Like all turtles, it is relatively unchanged since the time of dinosaurs.

Alligator—
The alligator's body is built for the swamp. Legs and feet allow it to move easily over the land; a streamlined body and powerful tail allow it to swim smoothly. The female pulls up water plants to build a nest on land. Fierce as she looks, she is a devoted mother. When a baby's grunts tell her that it is ready to hatch from the egg, she uncovers the nest and carries the hatchling to the water in her mouth.

Banded Pickerel—A slender fish with flat jaws like a duck's bill, this pickerel hovers among water-plant stems and roots. With a lightning-fast rush it grabs small fish and frogs for food.

Pig Frog—This large bullfrog rests on water plants when it's not hunting for food. Piglike grunts give it its name.

Fork-Tailed Bush Katydid—This katydid lives and feeds on the leaves of bushes and trees.

Pickerelweed—Growing in shallow water, this plant provides resting, hiding, and egg-laying places for swamp animals.

41

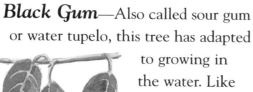

Black Gum—Also called sour gum or water tupelo, this tree has adapted to growing in the water. Like the cypress, its base is swollen for stability.

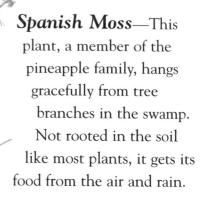

Spanish Moss—This plant, a member of the pineapple family, hangs gracefully from tree branches in the swamp. Not rooted in the soil like most plants, it gets its food from the air and rain.

Cottonmouth—This poisonous snake swims with its head above water. When disturbed, it opens its mouth, revealing the white lining for which it is named. Also called a water moccasin, it often basks in the sun during the day. At night, it hunts for frogs, small fish, snakes, and birds.

Killifish—This little fish, only 3 to 4 inches long, swims near the surface of the water, feeding on small plants and animals.

Florida Tree Snail—This snail lives on trees and eats algae off bark.

Green Tree Frog—This frog lives in the bushes and trees near water. During the day it sleeps on the undersides of large leaves or in damp shady places.

Fragrant Water Lily—Also called the scented pond lily, this floating plant grows in shallow water and provides a resting or hiding place for swamp animals. Many water snails and insects lay their eggs on the stems and under the leaves of this lily.

Great American Egret—A larger member of the heron family, this wading bird hunts in the shallow waters of the swamp.

Florida Panther—Paler than its mountain lion relatives, this panther lives on the many swamp islands, hunting deer. It is an endangered species because so much swampland has been destroyed by people.

Anhinga—
Also known as the water turkey or snake-bird, this large bird often perches on tree limbs with wings spread wide for drying. It swims on the water and spears fish with its long bill.

Florida Softshell—
This turtle has a soft shell covered by leathery skin. It is a fast swimmer with a powerful beak for catching prey. It frequently pokes its head just above the water, coming ashore only to lay eggs.

Barred Perch—This fish feeds on small fish and water animals. It grows up to 15 inches long.

Duckweed—At one-eighth to one-sixteenth of an inch wide, this water plant is the smallest flowering plant in the world. Air-filled sacs inside its leaflike body keep it afloat. It often forms dense mats over the water's surface and is a favorite food of water birds.

American Chameleon—
Also called the green anole, this is one of many lizards of the swamp. It lives among grasses, vines, and bushes, preying on insects. It can change from its usual green color to brown within seconds. During the spring and summer the female lays a single egg every fourteen days on the ground among leaf litter and moist debris.

Pine Woods Tree Frog—This frog generally lives and hunts in the treetops of pines near water. Like all frogs, the females lays eggs in the water.

SWAMP OF THE SOUTHEAST

GLOSSARY

adapt—to change, to adjust to the surroundings

algae—a group of one-celled plants having no true roots, stems, or leaves. Algae are usually found in moist places or in water

alpine—of high mountains

Arctic—the region of the earth north of the Arctic Circle, around the North Pole, where temperatures during the warmest months rise only to 50°F

bushel—a unit of measurement equaling eight gallons

cacti—a group of plants that have fleshy stems and branches with spines or scales instead of leaves

camouflage—a disguising or changing of appearance in order to hide

carnivore—a meat eater

desert—a region of the earth where the average rainfall is less than 10 inches per year, with plants and animals able to survive water scarcity

dormancy—a state in which animals or plants are inactive or sleeping and body processes slow down until difficult conditions, such as low temperatures or drought, improve

domestic—tame, not wild

environment—all the conditions surrounding and affecting the development of a plant, animal, or whole area

evaporate—to remove moisture from

fungi—a group of plants, including mushrooms, mildews, and molds, that have no leaves, flowers, or green color

habitat—the region where a particular plant or animal naturally grows or lives

hibernation—spending the winter in a dormant or resting state

insects—a group of animals without bones, with six legs and three divisions to their bodies

kelp forest—a region of ocean where cool, nutrient-rich waters allow giant sea kelp, the world's largest alga, to grow in abundance

larva—the developmental stage in many insects and animals that begins right after hatching

mammals—the group of animals in which the females feed the young with their milk

marine—living in the ocean

migrate—to travel from one region to another, as with the change of the seasons

nutrients—foods that contribute to good health or growth

nymph—a form of larva; young insect, not yet at the last or adult stage of development

pollen—the yellow, powderlike substance found on the male part (stamen) of a flower

pollinate—to place pollen on the female part (pistil) of a flower, so that the plant can reproduce

prairies—land regions where the average rainfall is between 10 and 30 inches and grasses are the dominant plant life

predator—an animal that hunts and kills for food

prey—an animal hunted or killed for food by another animal

rodents—a group of small animals such as mice, rats, squirrels, and rabbits with teeth for gnawing

salt marsh—a treeless, soft coastal wetland containing salt water

scavenger—any animal that eats rubbish and dead and rotting matter

seaweed—sea plants, especially sea algae

shellfish—any water animal with a shell, including clams, crabs, and lobsters

swamp—a type of wet, spongy land partially covered with water, where moss, shrubs, and some trees grow

taproot—the main root, usually growing straight down, from which smaller roots may branch out

tree line—the area beyond which trees cannot live

tundra—a treeless environment with a short growing season for other plants, severe winters, and low rainfall

North Pole

Arctic

ALASKA

Pacific Ocean

Alpine
Tundra ★

★ Prairie

Salt
Marsh

Atlantic
Ocean

★
Kelp Forest

UNITED STATES
OF AMERICA

★
Desert

★
Swamp